THE JAR SPELLS COMPENDIUM

A COLLECTION OF 60 MAGIC RECIPES TO MANIFEST ALL YOUR DESIRES FOR LOVE, PROTECTION, HEALTH, WELLNESS, GOOD LUCK, AND MORE

PAULA DERN

Disclaimer

This is not a manual of black magic and does not contain evil spells against other people, but only formulas to increase one's prosperity and well-being. The application of the advice in the book is total responsibility of the reader. Under no circumstances is the author responsible for the use of the contents of this book.

Table of Contents

Introduction 7

   Spell Jars: What Exactly Are They? 8

Chapter 1. All the Fundamentals 11

   Preparing Your Toolkit 11

   Making an Altar 15

   Casting a Circle 18

   Cleansing 20

   Intentions and Support 21

   Centering 22

   Grounding 24

Chapter 2. Raise Your Energy Before Conducting Spells ... 26

Chapter 3. Master the Art of Casting Jar Spells 28

   Set Up an Altar 28

   Preparing the Bath 29

   Defining Your Motives and Intentions 29

   Lighting Candles 30

   Meditating Before You Cast the Spell 31

Make or Chant a Prayer..32

Chapter 4. Jar Spell Recipes...*33*

Money and Prosperity Jar Spells..33

Spell to Create a Consciousness of Prosperity Spell........................ 33
Spell to Attract Prosperity 35
Cauldron Manifestation Spell 36
Money Powder 37
Riches Sigil 39
Money Grow Dressing Oil.. 40
Growing Riches Spell 42
Money Knot Spell 44
Prosperity Talisman 46
Pay Stub Growth Spell 48
Spell for Saving 49
Short Term Money Spell 50

Health and Wellness Spell Jar 53

To Heal the Body 53
Good Health Wish 55
Removing Negative Emotions 56
Healing Depression... 58
Healing Candle Spell 60
Conjuring Relief from Anxiety and Depression 62
Blocking Illness: a Protection Spell 63
Rapid Recovery: a Spell for Quick Healing...................................... 65
Hearty and Hale: a Spell to Improve Health 66

Planting Happiness Spell 68

Well-Being Anointing Oil 70

Ritual for Banishment of Internal Darkness 72

Mental Wellness Spell 73

Good luck Jar Spells..75

Spiritual Bath Spell for Good Luck 75

Road Opener Wiccan Candle Ritual... 76

'Bad Luck, Go Away!' Candle Spell to Remove a Curse 78

Good Luck & Prosperity Cinnamon Spell 79

Magic Sun Sigil... 80

Charge & Activate Talismans or Amulets 81

Good Luck Spell Chant: Janus' New Beginnings 82

Attract More Good Luck in the New Moon 84

Protection Jar Spells..86

Protecting Home and Heart 86

Safe Voyages: a Protection Spell for Travel...................................... 88

Avoiding Accidents: a Prevention Spell 89

Legal Relief: a Spell to Win a Court Case 91

Conjuring Peace: a Spell for a Happy Household 92

Vanquishing Visitors: a Spell to Get Rid of Unwanted Guests.......... 94

Under Your Thumb No More: a Spell to Free Yourself from Influence 96

Karmic Returns: a Spell to Reverse Evil Sent to You......................... 97

Love Jar Spells..100

Gimme Love Spell Jar 100

New Year, New Me Clarity Jar 101

Spell to Open Roads to Love 102

Self-Love & Spiritual Acceptance 104

Self-Love Bath 105

Getting Over Love Spell 107

Custom Love Sigil 109

Restore Love Knot Spell 110

Burning Heartbreak Spell 112

Mending Heartbreak Talisman 114

Charm for Attracting Quality Relationships 116

Romance Attraction Smudge 118

Stellar First Date Confidence Charm 119

Ritual Bath for a Blind Date 120

Rose Attraction Potion 122

Valentine's Day Jar Spell 124

Sugar Jar Love Spell 126

Lovers' Bind Rune 128

Sleep Jar Spells 129

Divining Dreams: a Spell for Good Sleep 129

Negating Nightmares: Another Spell for Good Sleep 130

Conclusion *132*

Introduction

Do you believe in magic? Do you believe that you can make something come true just by the power of your mind and soul? Have you heard of modern-day witches and want to learn and understand more about them? Well then, you are in the right place.

All of us are constantly wishing for things that we need or want, for situations to get better, or for the happiness of our loved ones. Well, wishing for something is only hope that your wishes come true. What if I told you, you could take an active part in making those wishes come true rather than relying on blind hope?

Your greatest asset is the power that you have within you. Your internal energy is what you can make use of to get what you want. Instead of hoping day and night that your wishes are fulfilled, you can take matters into your own hands right now.

By the law of equivalent exchange, if you put in a little effort, along with your faith, you can increase the chances of your thoughts and wants to become a reality. A bit of hard work on your part can help you achieve what you want in life.

Spell Jars: What Exactly Are They?

Sometimes also called *bottled spells or witch's jars*, these small glass bottles sealed with candle wax and capped with a cork or lid represent a magical tool used for protection, break a curse, or repel bad energies and magical attacks.

As indicated, in ancient times, they were usually filled with things like old rusty nails, razor blades, shards of glass, urine, and other objects with specific qualities and great magical potency, known in the Craft as catalysts.

They used to be buried or hidden near the maker's home in order to absorb the evil forces that had been sent to them. This is why a few centuries ago, it was completely normal for a family to have a bottle buried on their property for abundance and protection.

People who feared being already cursed might also choose to throw their jar into the fire, knowing that when the bottle exploded, it meant the spell had been broken. In other words, these charms were used as a form of protection or "counter magic," a means of blocking and trapping the harmful effects of witchcraft in different folk traditions.

But spell jars could also be used to make curses, not only to protect from them. In that case, part of the victim's (not maker's) urine, hair, or nail clippings, was placed in the bottle along with threads to simulate "traps." Other commonly used ingredients were seawater, dirt, sand, stones, knotted ropes, feathers, shells, herbs, flowers, salt, oil, or ashes. And again, also rusty nails, thorns, pieces of glass, wood, and bone.

Modern witches have begun using bottles for spells with the function of protection rather than making a curse.

This is why, nowadays, a spell jar is considered to be a tool specially prepared to stop any negativity.

Overall, it is used as a protective element of the home as its presence cancels evil spells, stops psychic attacks, annuls enemy conspiracies, unfair competition, hatred, friends with double standards, or mean family members.

It is also recommended to ward off misfortune, accidents, falls, or illnesses. In other words, it works as an absorbent sponge of negative energies, collecting any possible toxic element.

Overall, the most popular witch bottles are those intended for protection due to their high effectiveness. But at the same time, spell jars are also prepared to attract love, money, prosperity, etc.

Generally, modern witches put specific ingredients into the jar to match their intention. For example, a witch that wants to attract love will fill her bottle with things like red wine, lavender buds, apple slices, and rose quartz. Then, after consecrating the bottle with a spell, she may leave it in her bedroom to attract the lover of her dreams. Similarly, a bottle can also be placed in the room of someone sick to absorb their illness. Later, its contents are thrown out and buried to disperse it.

As indicated, according to tradition, once made, the bottle should be buried in the house's garden. However, nowadays, many people choose to hide it somewhere safe at home, place it in their bag or pour its contents into a river or sea to flow, just to name a few examples.

Overall, no matter if you wish to attract wealth, happiness, friendship, work, health, protection, intuition, or love... there are as many types of bottles as people who make them.

And by using plants and elements appropriate for the purpose you are specifically looking for, you can create a very effective tool to accomplish all your dreams.

I have provided you with a wide array of spells with varied purposes and uses. With a positive attitude, you can use these to fulfill your wishes. I hope you find what you are looking for in this book and wish you happy spell casting!

Chapter 1. All the Fundamentals

Preparing Your Toolkit

As with nearly all religious ceremonies, sacred objects are used to enhance the experience, convey certain messages to participants or to deities, and represent various intentions that are invoked during the ritual. Christian religions use particular vestments, depending on denomination, as well as altars and other symbols, typically speaking. Wicca is no different from this, and it too employs particular objects considered consecrated to the practitioners. These "tools," for lack of a better word, help Wiccans focus their intentions and maintain spiritual energy. The difference between Wiccan objects used in ritual and those used in monotheistic religions is that there is an acknowledgment that the Wiccan practitioners themselves provide the energy and sanctification of the objects, rather than being wholly directed by some specific higher power. It is more participatory and shared, rather than authoritative. Because of this, most objects used in Wiccan rituals are not merely symbolic: they are also practical and can be used within the physical realm for pragmatic purposes.

Before you hurry off to acquire each and every one of the tools listed below, remember that you need none of them to actually start to practice Wicca. Wiccan belief is as much about tapping into a sense of spiritual oneness with nature, regaining a sense of the cyclical reality of the world, and learning to channel your own energies with intention; the tools are devices to help you do this. Acquire them a few at a time, as you develop your practice and as need dictates. In addition, not all objects that one uses during the Wiccan ritual are actual tools: the symbols also play a role; plates of offering or other symbolic decorations are often employed; crystals, stones, herbs, and other significant objects to Wiccan practice are also present in ritual displays. That said, the following objects are frequently part of a Wiccan's toolkit to help them practice ritual, channel energy and intention and provide succor for the practitioner.

- Chalice: this symbol of fertility, representing the element of water and the renewing energy of the Mother Goddess herself, can have several roles in ritual. It can offer any kind of libation, such as wine or ale or water, depending on the ceremony (it is most certainly used in cakes and ale ceremony, a ritual feast emphasizing gratitude and the good things in life). It can also stand empty to symbolize the openness to the flow of energy from the universe. There are many elegant chalices from which to choose, but any vessel with which you endow energy is worthy of a chalice. Just be sure the material is of the earth, no artificial plastic.

- Wand: an oft-associated tool with witches, the wand is symbolic of the elemental power of air or fire. The object itself is not the source of power; rather, it is the conduit through which the practitioner channels her energy and makes real her intention. Traditionally made of wood (elder, oak, willow), a wand can be a homemade affair, carved by hand and consecrated with a gift to the tree that provided the wood. Natural material is preferred, of course, and if you live in an urban area, you can certainly seek out a wooden dowel to personalize and consecrate for your own.

- Pentacle: this ubiquitous object can be found at Wiccan and New Age shops and is used to charge other objects with energy; other tools are arranged on it in order to elevate their maximum power. The pentacle can also be mimed in the air, a ritual sign of protection. The pentacle is representative of all four elements of the physical world and their unity with the spiritual, making this a particularly powerful object.

- Athame: this is used to direct energy, either cutting away negative forces or encompassing the positive. Its masculine shape and power make it a symbolic representation of the god deity. It need not be particularly sharp, as the ritualistic ways in which it is used are symbolic rather than actual (no actual cutting, but presenting the action—exceptions are made for kitchen work or herbal preparations).

- Censer: the censer burns incense in order to purify the environment in which the ritual is practiced, as well as create an atmosphere wherein the mind's energy is focused on intention.

- Candles: the candle is central to all Wiccan practice and ritual, as a symbolic element in its own right. Representing the element of fire, primarily, the candle also channels the energy of the bonfire (community), the torch (sight), and ritual offerings (gratitude). It has always been sacred to rituals throughout the Western world. In addition, the candle is one of the most powerful tools in a Wiccan's toolkit, as it transmits the message or request (the intention) from the physical plane to the ethereal one. The flame burns, transmogrifying the physical object into the spiritual intention, blending the elements of earth, fire, and air to carry messages from one plane to another.

- Other: aside from the common items above, other objects often used in the Wiccan toolkit include the cauldron (where incense can be burned, offerings can be given, herbal potions can be brewed), the broom (to purify space, sweeping away negative energy), and the bell (to send clear messages into the ethereal plane). The bell, in particular, is used in religious rituals across the world, communicating faith or intention or congregation to those within the community.

Making an Altar

Once you have acquired your toolkit, you are ready to embark upon the symbolic centerpiece of the Wiccan ritual, the altar. Before you begin to build the altar, however, you will want to purify the space and/or participants: this can take the form of "smudging," burning particular herbs (usually sage or lavender) to clear a space of negative energy, or in ritual bathing for those who are participating (this might be particularly useful for an initiation ceremony, for example). Long-time practitioners of Wicca might keep a permanent altar in their home or place of worship, but even then, the altar will be adorned differently depending on the ritual, the celebration, and/or the time of year.

As the physical focal point of the Wiccan ritual, the altar is crucial to the exercise, and it also serves as a central force in any number of celebrations and practices throughout the year: celebrating Sabbats and Esbats (full moons), practicing meditation, saying prayers, or creating spells are all activities during which the altar can be a focal point. If you don't wish to create a permanent altar in your home, you can certainly set one up outside in a private, secluded space, or you can construct a small, moveable altar that can be put away after a ritual or ceremony is over. Practicing Wicca outdoors is a preference for many, as it allows you to communicate more closely with nature and the spiritual.

Many Wiccans prefer a round shape, both because of its feminine and egalitarian associations and for its practical use in creating the sacred circle. Additionally, as with other Wiccan tools, the ideal altar is made of natural materials—wood or stone, not plastic or other human-made material. Other than these basic requirements, the altar can be made of whatever you have on hand, an underused desk or a coffee or end table. It is not necessary to purchase something new, though if you intend to use your altar with any frequency, it might be a good idea to find one that you can use continuously, rather than having to clear it up and put it away frequently.

Once you have the surface of your altar, be sure to adorn it with whatever colors and decorations you feel give it a magical aura—this is the goal, of course, to transform an ordinary surface into an extraordinary place in which your intentions are heard and your rituals are successful. You can change this according to the seasons, of course, using browns and golds during autumn and greens and yellows during spring; always be in tune with natural cycles when you can. The altar is also a place to keep energy-channeling crystals or stones, images of deities or other symbolic representations, and candles. However, the main function of the altar during ritual is to hold your tools in some kind of thoughtful arrangement. As with all things Wiccan, this arrangement is mostly up to the individual practitioner, but there are a couple of standard arrangements that you can follow: first, a simple way to arrange your altar is to arrange all tools associated with the Mother Goddess (water and earth elements) to the left of center, while all tools associated with the Horned God or male deity (air and fire elements) to the right of center. Second, a more elaborate way of setting up an altar is to place the Goddess and God representations in the center with the rest of the tools arranged around them according to element and corresponding direction; that is, earth elements will be arranged facing north, while fire elements are arranged facing south, and water elements arranged to the west, with air elements arranged to the east. Again, many Wiccans will simply arrange their altar according to their own intuitive feeling, and you should feel free to do such, especially after you've had some time to practice and start to understand how energy works best for you.

The most important issue to remember when setting up your altar is that no one way is right or wrong, that no matter how large or small your area is, it is still meaningful. Indeed, you are the one to endow the space and the tools with energy and intention, so it should feel right for you. It should be a space of power, energy and serenity—and of practical use. If it's too crowded or if you cannot find what you need, then you know that it's not working as well as it could. In addition, each ritual need not be practiced on the same altar; a tree stump behind your home might serve particularly well for a harvest Sabbat, while your small home altar serves you better for daily meditation. The above are just some ideas to get you started.

Casting a Circle

Once you have your tools ready and your altar set up, it is time to cast a circle, a key component of each Wiccan ritual, be it for celebration, meditation, or any other ritual activity. Casting a circle around your space provides a boundary between your inner sanctum—the sacred space containing your tools, your altar, your physical self and any others participating—and the outside, ordinary world. Casting a circle is intended to create a magical space in which the ritual intention is realized.

While the altar is typically at the center of the circle, there are variations, of course. Just be sure to make the circle large enough so that nobody or no element steps outside of the boundary. The boundary can be marked with any number of items, such as stones or herbs or sea salt; the idea is to mark it with natural items containing spiritual energy. The circle should be a kind of portal to the spiritual world, bound by natural energies and forces. Not only does it form a kind of protective barrier, but it also psychologically prepares you for the ritual to come. See below for some basic steps to begin your ritual practice.

- Make sure your place is safe and practical, especially if you choose to practice outdoors. Being interrupted in the middle of a ritual is annoying at best and can be dangerous at worst.

- Be sure to purify that space via smudging or some other form of purification. Tidy up the space, if necessary, as well.

- Set your boundaries. Make sure the circle is large enough for what you need to do and include others when needed. Use the aforementioned natural materials to mark said boundary (salt, stones, herbs, etc.).

- Be sure that anything you will need for the ritual resides within the circle. Obviously, the altar with tools should be present, but consider anything else that might be necessary, such as offerings and specialized clothing. Set up the altar facing north, as you should also face that direction when beginning the ritual.

- Complete the circle by placing candles or other representative objects in each of the four cardinal directions: an earth element to the northernmost part of the circle, a fire element to the south, a water element in the west, and an air element to the east.

- Next, bless the circle: this can be as simple or as elaborate as your practice (or your coven) desires. It could be as simple as lighting a candle in each direction and blessing the spirits of north, south, west, and east, respectively.

- Indicate the purpose of the circle. Some traditions have you walk around the inside of the circle three times, invoking the spirits and stating your intended purpose. Hold the objects that represent the deities or the elements that you wish to invoke for your purpose and fill them with your energy.

- Meditate and/or complete your ritual.

- Finally, when your ritual is completed, close the circle. Give gratitude to whatever spirits, deities, and/or elements you have invoked, before removing each from their respective positions. Then, cast the circle in reverse to close it (if you placed your boundary moving north to south, then remove the boundary moving south to north). Closing the circle ensures that you have given proper thanks, as well as releasing the spirits for the time being.

Cleansing

Cleansing is often overlooked, but it's extremely important. It is the first step toward preparing your mind and body for gathering the energy needed for the spell itself. To cleanse means to remove the negative energy from something. Think of cleansing as the process in which you change from your work clothes after a day at the office into your relaxed, at-home gear. That shift in your mindset gets you ready to address different issues in a different environment. By cleansing your body and your workspace, you are setting aside the everyday distractions in order to focus on your spellwork.

In this step, you may take a bath or shower, meditate, do a bit of yoga, or simply sit with your eyes closed and breathe deeply for a couple of minutes. Let the noise and bustle of your everyday world fade away; focus only on the here and now, and your goal. Cleansing your space is equally important. Light a candle to signify the presence of light banishing darkness, or burn some incense to bring sympathetic energies to your work. Some spellcasters use a broom to symbolically sweep their workspace clean of distracting energy; or they sprinkle salt, saltwater, or blessed water to neutralize any negativity.

Intentions and Support

In terms of the actual ritual itself, this is largely up to you and your group (if participating) to decide. After the circle is cast, invocations are called for. Typically speaking, the Goddess and God will be invited into the circle first, followed by a recognition of each of the four elements and their contributions. Some ritual traditions also call for invoking the four cardinal directions. In yet others, a fifth element—Akasha, or Spirit—is also called upon. If you join a particular group, then they will likely already have their process in place, but if you are working on your own, decide what feels best for your intention.

Next, state your intention directly and clearly. Sometimes this will be quite simple, as for a Shabbat: "I am here to celebrate Samhain and to thank the Mother Goddess and the Horned God for a bountiful harvest," for example. Sometimes you will be asking for support, to help heal your mind or body, or you will be practicing spellwork with a particular purpose in mind. Be clear and specific in your intention, invoking which of the elements, spirits, and deities you need to thank or for assistance.

Once the intention is stated, the ritual itself can take many forms. There could be ritual singing or chanting, dancing or dramatic reenactments. For example, if you are performing a partnership ceremony or a Wiccan wedding, a dramatic reenactment of a spiritual union would be appropriate. Different groups have particular liturgical texts that they follow in order to best suit the intention or celebration. There may be offerings to hold up or to create within the sacred circle. If you are practicing solo, you may read from appropriate texts or chant your own compositions or perform acts of meditation or prayer. It isn't uncommon among certain Wiccan traditions to pray for the benefit of all of nature or humankind; the ritual dictates the boundaries of the intention.

Centering

Centering is a necessity in our lives and something that you may practice regularly without realizing it. The deep breaths you took before delivering a big speech in front of your class as a kid? That's centering. It's finding yourself in the waves of the ocean, and being able to confidently say, "I am right here right now, and all I have to do is row." Finding your center is about bringing all of the energy that is buzzing around your body to your core.

Finding your center is, both in life and in manifestation, pivotal. Centering ourselves can help us swim away from the waves of dissociation that are often felt with issues such as depression, anxiety, and stress. Centering brings us into the now of our bodies.

Offering yourself complete access to your energy is a necessity in any sort of spellwork because magic workings take energy.

Think of your core like a battery. It's charging, or draining, as you move through the world. Offer yourself time to discover what gives you energy. What do you draw energy from in your life? It could be anything, like swimming, dancing, sitting still, breathing or reading. Other activities, like doomscrolling or spending time with certain people, can drain your energy. It's perfectly fine to recognize what does and doesn't give you energy or make you feel good. Especially when it comes to people—family members, friends, lovers, and coworkers—knowing who energizes or drains you allows you to be intentional about how and when you spend time with them and how much energy you offer or expend when doing so.

You can also rely on outside sources, or structured activities, to center yourself. Is there music that makes you feel calm and refreshed? Soothing sounds can be a great way to feel the energy in the core of your body. If it ever feels difficult to get in touch with your core or challenging to channel your energy in an intentional way, meditating even for few minutes a day can help. Meditation allows you to feel incredibly present in the world around you.

Remember, only you can truly tap into and understand how your energy feels, as it is uniquely a part of you. Energy, and therefore the methods of centering, are different for everyone. Your special and diverse energies are not going to feel exactly like other people may describe their own. When centering, the goal is not to feel like someone else, or even feel something wildly different than usual. Rather, you're tuning into the world and into your body, and accessing your greater ability to manifest your personal magic.

Grounding

To ground oneself is to set foot in reality. It helps us remember that we are very real and worthy of recognizing our place in this world. That doesn't mean the earthly world is not inherently magical—life is magic—and we must recognize the divine magic of our lives in acts like eating, bathing, and stretching. Those are all aspects of grounding. Grounding is a rejuvenating celebration of the event that is your existence. It connects us to the element of earth and makes us feel protected and stable. A connection to the physical world can bring us joy, and offers a view of our current abundance, allowing us to see with greater clarity the possible doorways to even more abundance. There are a lot of ways to practice grounding, but one of my personal favorites is an intentional indulgence, such as enjoying cake and ale. In the best way, rituals can drain your energy, and offering yourself nourishment that your body both needs and deserves gives you a moment to rejoice, rather than sinking into the lull of tired discontentment.

Some people decide that they must always be in the astral plane and use their incredibly vivid imaginations to keep themselves ungrounded. Some people crave so much to be spiritually attuned or gifted that they will do anything, like convincing themselves that they are guided by the spirit of Tutankhamun's wet nurse while wearing a muumuu and enough crystals to fill a three-foot-deep swimming pool. Some may be so ungrounded as to be easily coaxed into ideologies that can be dangerous for them and the world around them. Remaining grounded in the mundane world allows us to make the most of our here and now. While reincarnation is a real possibility, we should offer this life the respect it deserves by being present in it whenever possible and exploring our spiritual world when we feel safe and ready to connect.

Chapter 2. Raise Your Energy Before Conducting Spells

Let's begin with the question, *"What is energy?"*

You are surrounded by energy. Everything is made out of energy! You are a source of energy. Your ideas are made up of energy. Everything you perceive is made out of energy. When you comprehend how strong and mystical energy is, it's truly rather amazing.

When we talk about "negative energy" in the spiritual sense, we're talking about undesired energy or energy that doesn't make us feel good. Have you ever stepped into a location and sensed something wasn't quite right?

We all have various perspectives on life! What you see as negative energy may be perceived as good energy by someone else. Always pay attention to your gut sensations or intuition. When you sense that the energy in a location or around a certain individual is off, pay attention to the clues your body is sending to you.

Bad emotions (sadness, rage, envy, irritation, etc.) are only some of the things that may cause negative energy to stay in a location. Where there has been a death, wherever there has been any form of violence, a disagreement or a brawl, sickness or ailment might give you a lot of negative energy too.

It's usually a good idea to purify the area before executing a spell or ritual. This should be performed whether or not you perceive bad energy since not all bad energy is really negative...if that makes sense. Some energy is just unwelcome! For example, if you cast a love spell on Monday and then choose to do money magic on Tuesday in the same spot, the love spell's energy may still be there. This may perplex the cosmos and make manifesting your wishes more difficult.

Witchcraft is a deeply personal path to take. We all practice and develop specific standards of behavior that best suit our personalities over time, but one thing we all have in common is that when we sense that the power in space is off, we instantly grab our sage, incense, selenite crystal or whatever cleansing tools we prefer to use to clear the space of that unwanted energy. There are two advantages of purifying a place before a spell or ritual. It will be clear of any unwelcome energy. This will make it easier for you to explain your objectives. Plus, you'll feel more at ease knowing that any negative energy has been removed from your environment.

Chapter 3. Master the Art of Casting Jar Spells

After learning the fundamentals of spells and rituals, you might eventually want to try your hand at crafting your own. This will strengthen your manifestation skills, foster your connection to witchcraft, and deepen your connection to the spiritual world and energies that surround you. Following is a simple breakdown and guidelines on how to get started crafting your own spells and rituals.

Set Up an Altar

You do not necessarily need an altar to perform a ritual or cast a spell, but having one is beneficial. Some spellcasters choose not to have altars but don't have a problem with casting their spells. A few spellcasters use their tables or any other surface at home to cast spells. They use a clean, white cloth to cover the surface before they cast the spell. Some choose to sit on the floor instead.

If you look for spells online, you will be asked to sit at an altar before you cast a spell. Why do you think this is important? Before you perform any magic, you need to create a sacred space for yourself to manifest your intent using magic.

Preparing the Bath

You need to cleanse yourself of any negative energy before you cast spells, and the best way to remove the energy is to take a ritual bath. This enables you to prepare yourself physically and mentally before you cast the spell or perform rituals. A daily shower does not keep your body fresh and clean, and for this reason, you need to use a ritual bath to calm your body and mind. Not every magic circle will ask you to begin with casting a protection circle, but it is best to draw one around you before you cast spells. This will prevent the entry or movement of bad or negative energy from around you into the circle. You can also prepare yourself mentally through a ritual bath.

Defining Your Motives and Intentions

As mentioned earlier, your intentions are very important when it comes to casting spells. You need to know what your intent is and what your end goal is. It is important to be specific when you work with energies. Do not be general because it can add some confusion to the spell. Avoid using negative phrases, sentences, and words in your spell.

You should have good intentions when you cast a spell. Your intent should not affect anybody and should be for your happiness. Having said that, you should understand that spells you cast will affect those around you, so ensure your spell does not harm anybody around you. Only when your thoughts and intentions are pure can your spell work. There can be no negativity in your mind when you cast the spell.

To do this, write your intentions and thoughts down on a piece of paper or in your spiritual journal. This is a great way to frame your desires and use the right words when you cast a spell. As you write it down, you should describe your innermost desire with meaningful and clear words. This will help you understand your wants and needs better. Do not use the phrase 'I want' when you send messages through a spell. It is best to say you are grateful for everything you have.

Lighting Candles

Most spells you cast require the use of candles. If you do choose one such spell, you should light it only when you have determined and worded your intent. Place this candle on the altar before you light it. When you do this, it indicates to the universe you are ready to change some aspect of your life. In the realm of magic, a candle is used because it has a connection to the spiritual world.

Different parts of the candle represent different elements in the universe:

- The wax is associated with nature and represents the earth element.

- The hot wax dripping and melting on the side of the candle represents the water element.

- The smoke is associated with the air element.

- Lastly, the flame is associated with purity and represents the fire element.

It is both enlightening and beneficial to use candles when you perform any ritual. Candles not only refresh your mood and change your mindset but also enhance the power of the spell you want to cast. The color of the candle and its flame will attract different types of energies depending on the type of spell you want to cast and your intent. Candles have healing powers and are the main ingredient in any spell you cast, and the color you choose depends on your intent and circumstance.

Meditating Before You Cast the Spell

This is an important part of any spell casting ritual. You should focus on your intent before you begin the spell. The best way to do this is through meditation.

Before you meditate, you need to empty your mind so you can focus only on your intent. This is important if you want your spell to work. According to an experienced spellcaster, meditation is very important if you want to cast spells. You cannot expect the spell to work simply because you use an altar, place all the ingredients on the altar, and pray with candles. The most important aspect is to concentrate on your objective or intent before you cast a spell.

When you perform a spell, you should focus on your goal. This intent and focus will transform into energy. So, don't be doubtful or afraid of what may happen. You also should rid yourself of any negative emotions. The energy you put out into the universe will be scattered and weak before the session ends if you let negativity seep in.

Make or Chant a Prayer

Once you focus on your intents, visualize, and meditate, cast the spell. Chant the words you have written down by saying a few words. When you do this, you can send your message to the universe. All you need to do then is to trust the universe will grant your wish. Be very specific about your intent if you want the spell to work for you.

Once you are done with the spell, thank the universe for listening to what you must say.

Chapter 4. Jar Spell Recipes

Money and Prosperity Jar Spells

Spell to Create a Consciousness of Prosperity Spell

Before you can attract wealth, you have to feel that you are worthy of it. Many of us have been taught to believe we do not deserve prosperity, but those ideas can hinder our ability to achieve financial security.

You will need:

- 14 green votive candles
- Pine Essential Oil
- 1 empty glass container
- A piece of paper

Instructions:

1. The first night of this spell should be a new moon.
2. Anoint and dress the green candles with the pine essential oil.

3. Write your affirmations (desires) on the piece of paper.

4. On the night of the new moon, light one of the candles. While it is burning, read your affirmation aloud. Focus on the feeling that it is already done, that your affirmation has already been met.

5. After approximately 5 minutes, snuff the candle. Rub your hands in the smoke and waft the smoke toward your face, your body, and your clothes. Lock that scent into your mind so you associate the scent with abundance, prosperity, and your belief.

6. Repeat this ritual each day for the next 13 days, using a new candle each time.

7. Keep the spent candles with each other and separate from the unused candles.

8. On the night of the full moon, after having performed this spell for fourteen straight days, light all fourteen candles again (all together). Let the candles burn themselves out.

9. Collect the remnants of the candles and place them in the glass jar. Also, place your written affirmation into the jar.

10. Bury the jar in the front yard of your home.

Spell to Attract Prosperity

This prosperity spell can be used for any kind of prosperity—financial gain or prosperity in the fullness of inner peace, the source of all true prosperity.

You will need:

- 1 green candle
- 1 sprig of white sage
- A pinch of cinnamon
- A cauldron or metal bowl

Instructions:

1. On the night of the new moon, put the green candle and the white sage in the cauldron or bowl.
2. Light both the candle and the sage.
3. Sprinkle cinnamon into the flame of the candle. While you do so, recite the following, *"I embrace prosperity and inner peace."*
4. Repeat these words and keep sprinkling cinnamon into the flame until the cinnamon is gone.

Cauldron Manifestation Spell

There are times when your desired manifestation may take longer than others. Do not be discouraged. Remember that the universe will provide in its own time. While you wait, try this spell to nurture your wish and bring it to fruition.

You will need:

- 1 piece of paper
- A pair of scissors
- A cauldron or metal bowl
- A pinch of powdered ginger
- 1 capsule or tablet of 'Blessed Thistle'
- A piece of green cloth

Instructions:

1. Cut the sheet of paper into 12 strips. On one strip, write your wish in the form of an affirmation.
2. Fold the paper trip three times and put it in the cauldron.
3. Sprinkle the powdered ginger in the cauldron, along with the broken Blessed Thistle herbal supplement.

4. Cover the cauldron or bowl with the green cloth.

5. Let the cauldron or bowl sit overnight.

6. In the morning, remove the cloth and repeat the spell.

7. Continue in this manner for a total of 12 days.

If your desire has not yet materialized by the time of the full moon, take a break from the spell during the waning moon and begin again on the first day of the waxing moon. Do not give up! Trust that the universe will provide when the time is right.

Money Powder

This powder is great for improving any kind of financial situation. Sprinkle it around yourself to invite more money to come to you at home, at work or while gambling. You can also burn money powder on a charcoal disc on a heat-proof dish to increase the power of other prosperity and money spells.

When to perform this spell:

On a Thursday or during a waxing moon

Time to allot for the spell:

15 minutes

Where to perform the spell:

Altar or kitchen

You will need:

- Mortar and pestle or grinder
- 1 tablespoon dried chamomile
- 1 tablespoon cinnamon
- 1 tablespoon dried cloves
- 1 tablespoon dried parsley
- Funnel
- Glass vial or jar with a lid

Instructions:

1. Cleanse your altar or kitchen space.
2. With the mortar and pestle, grind the chamomile, cinnamon, cloves, and parsley, setting a specific intention to attract money into your life.
3. As you grind the mixture into a powder, say the following four times: "Growing riches, sprouting funds."
4. Use a funnel to pour the powdered herbs into a glass vial.
5. Your powder is charged and ready for use.

Riches Sigil

Creating a custom money sigil can help you attract wealth and riches. To get started with this simple spell, all you need is your imagination, intention, and something to write with. Using a green pen will help elevate your spell.

When to perform this spell:

On a Sunday, Thursday, or during a waxing or new moon

Time to allot for the spell:

10 minutes

Where to perform the spell:

Altar

You will need:

- Pen with green ink
- 2 sheets of paper

Instructions:

1. Cleanse your altar.

2. Use a green pen to write the phrase Bring me riches on the first sheet of paper. Focus on your intentions.

3. Deconstruct the letters of the phrase into basic strokes, like curves, dots, dashes, and lines. Draw these strokes below the phrase on the same paper.

4. On the same sheet of paper, combine the strokes to form the outline of a shape. This could be a square, a heart, a cross, or a triangle. Place any remaining circles, arcs, and dashes along the lines or around the shape. This shape is your money sigil.

5. Redraw your money sigil, now coded with your intentions, on the second sheet of paper. Carry it with you.

Money Grow Dressing Oil

Do you wish that you could multiply your money? You can rub this oil mixture on your skin to help you stay focused so you can improve your finances. Remember to do a patch test first if you have sensitive skin. You can also dress your candles or tools with this oil to enhance the power of other money spells.

When to perform this spell:

On a Thursday or during a waxing moon

Time to allot for the spell:

15 minutes

Where to perform the spell:

Altar

You will need:

- Small amber roller bottle or dropper bottle
- 2 tablespoons carrier oil, such as almond or jojoba
- 2 drops ginger essential oil
- 2 drops sandalwood essential oil
- 1 drop bergamot essential oil
- 1 drop patchouli essential oil
- 1 bay leaf
- 1 tablespoon cinnamon chips

Instructions:

1. Cleanse your altar.
2. Pour the carrier oil into an amber roller bottle.

3. Add the ginger, sandalwood, bergamot, and patchouli essential oils, one at a time. As you add each ingredient, chant the phrase "Money, grow and multiply."

4. Add the bay leaf and cinnamon chips.

5. Hold the bottle in your hands and envision energy wrapping around it. Charge it with your intentions.

6. Gently shake the bottle before each use to ensure the elements are combined. Use the oil on your skin, charms, or other objects.

Growing Riches Spell

This spell uses Money Grow Dressing Oil and a mint plant, which you can buy at any grocery store that sells herbs. Mint is very useful for attracting money and has a variety of uses. A mint plant is a valuable investment for any witch.

When to perform this spell:

During a new moon

Time to allot for the spell:

15 minutes

Where to perform the spell:

Altar or kitchen

You will need:

- Mint plant
- 4 items that represent each of the four elements (e.g., a bowl of water, soil, a candle, and a besom)
- Coin or money charm
- Money Grow Dressing Oil

Instructions:

1. Cleanse your altar or kitchen space.

2. Place your new mint plant on your altar and spend time consecrating it. To consecrate the mint plant, pass it through your four elements or ask the elements to assist with consecrating. Both methods utilize your desire to purify, charge, and bless. You can use words or think silently about your goals.

3. When you are finished, anoint the coin or charm with Money Grow Dressing Oil to charge it for use. Place it near the base of the mint plant.

4. Close your eyes and meditate on your intention for the mint plant to grow and attract money.

5. You can pick the anointed mint leaves and carry them as a charm or use them in other money spells.

Money Knot Spell

This knot spell stores and binds your intention to attract money in every knot you tie. You can use any combination of money herbs as incense in this spell, including basil, bay leaf, chamomile, cinnamon, clove, dill, or ginger.

When to perform this spell:

On a Thursday or during a full moon or waxing moon

Time to allot for the spell:

30 minutes

Where to perform the spell:

Altar

You will need:

- Lighter or matches
- Money Powder or a powdered blend of any money herbs
- Charcoal disc

- Heat-proof dish
- 3 green tea light candles
- 1 (12-inch) piece of green, gold, or white string

Instructions:

1. Cleanse your altar.
2. Burn the Money Powder on a charcoal disc on a heat-proof dish and arrange the tea light candles in a triangular configuration.
3. Light the candles and focus on your intention of generating more money.
4. Tie five knots in your string. As you tie each knot, say:

    "With knot one, the spell has begun,

    with knot two, the spell will come true,

    with knot three, the spell hears my plea,

    with knot four, the spell grows more,

    with knot five, the spell is alive."

5. Allow the tea light candles to continue burning while you meditate for 15 minutes, visualizing what you want to manifest.

Prosperity Talisman

This spell will consecrate and charge a piece of jewelry with your intentions of prosperity and wealth. This particular version uses a necklace, but you may alter it for any piece of jewelry, crystal, stone or another pendant of choice. To amplify the spell, use a necklace made with crystal or wood. Wear it under your clothes, hidden from others.

When to perform this spell:

On a Sunday or during a new moon

Time to allot for the spell:

15 minutes

Where to perform the spell:

Altar

You will need:

- Necklace
- Pinch of dried mint

- White or green votive or pillar candle
- Lighter or matches

Instructions:

1. Cleanse your altar.
2. Purify the necklace.
3. Sprinkle the dried mint on the top of the candle.
4. Light the candle and focus on visualizing its money properties.
5. Move your necklace through the smoke and say: "Necklace I charge with prosperity, attract to me riches and wealth, and serve me well with sincerity while you're worn in secret stealth."
6. Allow some of your power to infuse the object, charging it for use.
7. You may use the same candle to repeat the spell every few months.

Pay Stub Growth Spell

Bless and grow your pay stub. This may very well be the safest and least obtrusive path to using magic to increase your prosperity.

You will need:

- Your pay stub
- A seedling
- Garden soil
- A small plant pot

Instructions:

1. Put the garden soil into the plant pot.
2. Dig into the garden soil and "plant" your pay stub. As you do, recite the following: *"The fruit of my work, the seed which I plant. Grow seed grow. Your fruit is so sweet."*
3. Plant the seedling on top of the pay stub.
4. Nurture and care for this plant throughout the growing season.

Spell for Saving

Some people find saving to be a simple and obvious concept to put into practice, while others can not hold onto that last dime in their pocket. The first thing you will need to do is to go to a bank and open a savings account. Then, write a plan detailing how you will save (how frequently you will contribute; how much you will contribute; how you will make that happen, etc.). Remember that magic works with real-world action, not instead of it.

You will need:

- A few stones (anything found in nature that appeals to you)
- A brown cord
- A statement/printout from your savings account

Instructions:

1. Cast a sacred circle.
2. When you consecrate the elements, include the stones in the Earth consecration, by putting them in the salt dish
3. Consecrate the cords by the four elements and recite the following: *"Air and Fire. Water and Earth. Consecrate this tool of magic that binds me to the commitment I make."*

4. Now consecrate the bank statement by the four elements, and say: *"Air and Fire. Water and Earth. Consecrate this tool of finance that holds and keeps the commitment I make."*

5. Stand within the sacred circle and rub them over your body, from head to toe. Feel yourself grounded and connected to Earth as you do so.

6. Visualize trunks full of buried treasure, and gold mines, and any other ways that Earth helps us hold, save, and store treasure.

7. Hold the statement in your non-dominant hand. Use the cord to bind the statement to you. As you do so, recite the following: *"I am bound to save. So mote it be."*

8. Close the sacred circle.

Short Term Money Spell

Money is just one of those life necessities, whether we like it or not. It is simply a fact of life. Like any life necessity, a spell can easily aid in the process of acquiring what you need. This spell can assist you in gaining that quick infusion of money when you are going to be a bit short.

You will need:

- Cinnamon Incense

- A small bowl of sea or mineral salt
- A small bowl of moon water
- 1 Red Candle
- Dried Basil
- 1 Citrine crystal
- Fingernail or hair clippings
- A coin from the year of your birth (avoid pennies)
- A token that represents your work to you
- 1 green sachet
- A length of brown string

Instructions:

1. Cast a protective circle.
2. Light the red candle and begin to burn the incense.
3. Ground and Center your energy.
4. Meditation and visualization play key roles in the success of this spell. Meditate and visualize your life when the money you want is already with you. Let that sense of calm confidence wash over you. Focus on every detail that

you visualize—how you feel after getting the money, how you spend the money, what this money does for you in your life.

5. Rinse the Citrine in flowing water. As you add ingredients to the sachet, pass the item through the incense smoke, and then place the items in the bag.

6. When all of the items have been added to the bag, tie the sachet closed with the length of brown string.

7. Sprinkle the outside of the sachet with the salt.

8. Spritz the outside of the sachet with the moon water.

9. While holding the sachet in your dominant hand, recite the following: *"Money is the thing I need. The act is pure in heart and deed. I ask that you grant all to me. Smile your smile of gold. So mote it be."*

10. Allow the red candle to burn itself out.

11. Close the sacred circle.

12. Keep the sachet nearby (in a pocket, in a purse, in a briefcase, etc.)

Health and Wellness Spell Jar

To Heal the Body

This spell hones in on the malady or pain that is affecting your body, whether that malady is physical, emotional, or spiritual.

You will need:

- A large piece of paper
- Yellow, purple, and red felt-tipped pens
- A black marker pen

Instructions:

1. The first thing that you are going to do is take your large piece of paper and draw three concentric circles on it.

2. Use the felt-tipped pens to color the concentric circles. The inner circle should be purple. The middle circle should be yellow and the outer one red.

3. Now above the three concentric circles, add another circle. Below the concentric circles, draw two lines. This way, the concentric circles represent your body, the circle above indicates your head and the two lines below the concentric circles represent your legs.

4. Now think of the pain that you are feeling. This could be physical, emotional, or spiritual pain. Take out your black marker and place a dot on the region that represents your pain. Here are what each of the regions in the concentric circles represents.

5. Red represents physical pain

6. Yellow represents the emotional distress or discomfort that you are enduring

7. Purple focuses on spiritual maladies

8. Once you know the regions, you can place a dot in the respective region, depending on the type of pain you are feeling. Each time you place a dot, speak these words: "Raphael, Raphael Angel of ease

    Help me to understand this pain, please.

9. Now sit quietly and absorb the color that you have marked into your body. If you have marked all three colors, then absorb them one by one.

10. When you have absorbed one color, visualize a white light entering your body as well. This white light is going to clear out the color from your body, in turn helping you deal with the problem.

11. You have to perform this ritual for the next two days.

12. At the end of those two days, you might be able to better understand the cause of the trauma.

NOTE: Remember that this ritual is not a replacement for actual medical diagnosis. Though it might bring about healing effects to your body, it does not get rid of the problem entirely. Make sure that you get medical attention wherever you see fit.

Good Health Wish

This is a simple spell that is best performed during the phase of the New Moon.

You will need:

- 3 bay leaves
- A piece of paper
- Pen

Instructions:

1. During the New Moon, write down your wish for good health. Visualize what happens when the wish comes true. Imagine yourself enjoying life with a good spirit.

2. Fold the paper into thirds, making sure that the bay leaves are placed inside.

3. Bring the paper close to your heart and visualize the wish coming true again.

4. One gain, fold the paper in thirds.

5. Keep the paper in a dark place, such as a closet or a drawer.

6. Every night, before you head to bed, visualize the wish coming true.

7. When the wish does come true and you are in good health, burn the paper as a way of saying thanks.

Removing Negative Emotions

When you are overwhelmed by negative emotions, then you can make use of the rather simple spell to get rid of them.

You will need:

- A dark stone

Instructions:

1. Lie down comfortably on the ground or floor. You can choose to be close to your altar or any other space that is comfortable for you.

2. Close your eyes and imagine that there is a circle of white light surrounding you.

3. Take the stone and place it above your solar plexus.

4. Imagine that all your negative emotions are flowing into the stone. Imagine your anger, envy, deep-rooted resentments, and other emotions being absorbed by the stone.

5. Try to focus on one emotion at a time. If the emotion is anger, then imagine a red energy exiting your body and getting absorbed by the stone. If it is envy, then imagine a yellow energy. This way, give a color to each of the negative emotions.

6. Once you have transferred all of your negative energies into the stone, place it over your head so that you can gain clarity about these emotions or energies.

7. Place the stone over your heart.

8. Recite the verse below clearly: "With this stone

    Negative be gone,

    Let water cleanse it

    Back where it belongs."

9. Once you have recited the above verse, take the stone outside and bring it to a source of running water, such as a river or a stream. Toss the stone inside. You can also throw it out into the open sea or a lake.

10. If no sources of water are near you, then you can hurl the stone as far away from you as possible.

Healing Depression

Never should you assume that spells can be a replacement for proper medical care. Depression is a serious condition and despite the fact that this spell can bring relief to you, it is not a permanent solution. I would still recommend that you consult with a doctor and find a solution that helps you in the long term.

You will need:

- A red pouch or a talisman bag
- If you are a man, then pick a piece of pine cone
- If you are a woman, then pick a piece of angelica root
- A sprig of rosemary
- White candle
- A lucky token or coin

- A dog tag

- Clary sage oil which you will use to dress the objects

- Clary sage incense

- A pin or a burin

Instructions:

1. One of the best parts of this ritual is that you can perform it on yourself or for somebody else.

2. If you or the person the ritual is focused on are male, then write down the name of the person on the pine cone.

3. If you or the person the ritual is focused on are female, then write down the name of the person on the angelica root.

4. When you have chosen the lucky token or coin, make sure that it is a representation of the person. In other words, it should be something that reminds you of the person. If you are focusing on yourself, then use an object that you feel links to you.

5. Once you have the token in your hands, say the below line:

    "May this good luck token come with healing to [the individual's name]."

6. Now inscribe the name of the person (if it is yourself, then your name) on the dog tag. As you are writing down the name, go over the above words again.

7. Set the items in a pouch

8. Set some oil to the bag for dropping

9. Now use the oil to anoint the token and dog tag, then place these items in the pouch or the bag. Seal the bag or pouch tightly.

10. Light up the incense and keep the bag in the smoke.

11. Light up the candle next and pass the bag over the flame of the candle.

12. If you have performed the ritual for yourself, then keep the bag with you for at least a week. If you have performed the ritual for someone else, then present the bag to them and tell them to keep it with them or close to them for a minimum of 7 days.

Healing Candle Spell

You will need:

- A blue, white, or yellow candle

- Healing Oil: angelica, comfrey, and chamomile

- A small, thin paintbrush

- A dish or candleholder

- Matches

- Tibetan healing incense

- An incense holder

- A small knife, or screw

Instructions:

1. Cast your circle and anoint the candle. With the small knife or screw tip, carve the words "heal me" on both sides of the candle, then light the candle. Light the incense and allow the smoke to drift across the candle flame, filling the room with a healing scent. (Place the incense far enough away from you so that you are not directly breathing the line of smoke).

2. Allow your mind to drift into an alpha state: your gaze is out of focus, your mind is calm, and thoughts are discarded as they enter the space of your mind. As the candle burns, know that you are in the right place for healing of the spirit, mind, body, and soul. Feel the benevolent energy fill your

circle. Feel the power of the universe filling your circle with healing light.

3. When you are ready, open the circle and ground. Allow the candle and incense to burn down.

Conjuring Relief from Anxiety and Depression

This spell can be used for either anxiety, which boils down to a fear of the future, or depression, which often indicates being stuck in the regrets of the past. The ritual is the same for either, though the signifying colors of the candle are distinct.

When to Perform:

Any time during the waning moon

How long it takes:

As long as it takes the candles to burn down over the course of nine days

You will need:

- 1 white pillar candle for anxiety OR
- 1 red pillar candle for depression
- Orange essential oil
- Crystal or stone (optional)

Instructions:

1. Smudge your space well: you want your energy to be clear and fresh.

2. Place your candle in the center of the altar and anoint it with orange essential oil. This replaces anxiety or depression with strength and vitality. The white candle is to purify your mind of anxiety, while the red candle fortifies you with courage.

3. Light the candle and, if you like, choose a particular crystal or stone to pass through the flame, drawing symbolic energy to you (a moonstone for peace, perhaps, or a bloodstone for courage). As the candle burns, recite your incantation: *"My power of self is so clearly strong, that no worries or troubles can come along. I cast protection against these worries in my soul because might is my weapon and harmony is my goal."*

4. Let the candle burn for a few minutes as you meditate on peacefulness and strength, then snuff it. Repeat this ritual each day at the same time for nine consecutive days.

Blocking Illness: a Protection Spell

Most people who practice magic acquire a repertoire of healing and protective tools, including amulets, sachets, potions, and spells.

Herbs, in particular, are key to most healing rituals and can be used in a variety of combinations for a myriad of results. Here is a general health spell using candles: you can amplify its power or specify its intentions with the addition of particular herbal oils or dried herbs, depending on your needs.

When to Perform:

During a full moon

How long it takes:

As long as it takes the candles to burn down

You will need:

- 1 white taper candle
- 1 indigo taper candle
- 1 purple taper candle

Instructions:

1. Smudge your space with a mix of sage and rosemary for maximum protection and cleansing.
2. Arrange your candles in a triangle with the white "self" candle at the apex. The indigo represents physical health, while the purple candle symbolizes spiritual well-being.
3. Call upon each of the elements to aid in protection: *"I call upon the earth to keep me grounded. I call upon the fire to*

purge me of fever. I call upon the water to wash away the infection. I call upon the wind to whisk away bad energies."

4. Let the candles burn all the way down, and when the wax remnants are cool, keep them under your pillow until the next full moon, then bury them beneath a strong and sturdy tree.

Rapid Recovery: a Spell for Quick Healing

This spell is appropriate for a particular wound or illness. While the previous spell is, at its core, a protection spell, this is a more focused conjuring. It may not be powerful enough to heal chronic conditions, but I have used it to good effect when dealing with sprained ankles and head colds.

When to Perform:

Any time it's needed

How long it takes:

As long as it takes the candle to burn down

You will need:

- 1 white taper candle
- Eucalyptus essential oil
- Black cord or string

Instructions:

1. Cleanse your space and set your candle at the center of your altar.

2. Anoint the candle with the healing and cleansing eucalyptus oil. Use the cord or string to tie around the injured or ill part of the body, as close to the area as you can.

3. Light the candle and state your intention: *"Close this wound, end the sick, make me healthy, sure and quick."*

4. Let the candle burn down, untying the cord and letting it burn—use caution. In the last moments of the dying flame, imagine the injury or illness being consumed by the flame. Be sure to get rid of remnants directly, sending them far away.

Hearty and Hale: a Spell to Improve Health

This spell uses candle magic in a slightly different way: you are focusing your magic on your homemade incense blend, using the candle to release the scents and energies into the atmosphere. This incense blend can also be brewed into a tea, assuming that you've used kitchen-grade products safe for consumption.

When to Perform:

During a full moon

How long it takes:

A couple of hours (mostly inactive)

You will need:

- Incense ingredients: dried orange peel, caraway seeds, black peppercorns, dried sage, rosemary, cinnamon, and natural sugar (such as demerara)
- 1 orange or red tea candle
- Flameproof incense burner or other vessels

Instructions:

1. This is best prepared in the kitchen, so smudge the kitchen with a strong sage bundle.
2. Prepare your incense mixture by combining one tablespoon each of dried orange peel for vitality, caraway seeds for antiseptic properties, black peppercorns for endurance, sage for mental strength, rosemary for memory, cinnamon for physical strength, and sugar for sweetness (of life).
3. Put your ingredients in an incense burner or other flameproof container and light your tea candle underneath the incense, releasing its scents and intentions into the room.
4. Let it burn until it's spent, then bury the remnants in a place where healthy plants grow.

Planting Happiness Spell

Happiness is often just within reach, but not quite within our grasp. Cast this spell to radiate happiness that will leave you glowing and feeling in sync with the moment. In this spell, you'll plant a tree or shrub, which will allow you to find happiness in nature.

When to perform this spell:

On a Wednesday or Sunday

Time to allot for the spell:

45 minutes

Where to perform the spell:

Outdoors

You will need:

- Shielding Mist (optional)
- Shovel
- Plant or tree
- 5 clear quartz crystals

- Gardening gloves (optional)

- Shovel

- Water (enough to water your plant—the amount varies from plant to plant, so do your research!)

- Dash salt

Instructions:

1. Use your intuition to choose an outdoor spot (e.g., somewhere in your garden) for your happiness plant or tree.

2. Cleanse the chosen area. If you'd like to, spray it with Shielding Mist.

3. Use the tip of the shovel to scratch out a pentagram shape in the earth that encompasses you and your plant.

4. Place the clear quartz crystals at the points of the pentagram.

5. Begin digging a hole in the soil. Wear gardening gloves if you'd like.

6. Place your plant or tree in the hole. Pack dirt up to the base of the plant to stabilize it.

7. Spend 10 minutes meditating silently next to the plant, reaching out with your consciousness to connect with its energy. While meditating, say: "Plant of happiness,

   fill my life,

   brighten my heart,

   and lift my spirit."

8. Water your plant and sprinkle the salt as an offering in the surrounding area.

9. Care for your plant weekly, repeating your meditation and chant.

Well-Being Anointing Oil

In this spell, you'll blend, charge, and bless this magical anointing oil. Use this oil on objects, in well-being spells, or on your pulse points as a way to amplify your intentions to attract positivity into your life. If applying to your skin, remember to do a patch test.

When to perform this spell:

During a new or full moon

Time to allot for the spell:

20 minutes

Where to perform the spell:

Altar or kitchen

You will need:

- Small amber roller bottle or dropper bottle
- 1 tablespoon carrier oil, such as jojoba or almond oil
- 2 drops patchouli essential oil
- 2 drops lavender essential oil
- 2 drops ylang-ylang essential oil
- 1 teaspoon dried chamomile

Instructions:

1. Cleanse your altar.
2. Add the carrier oil to an amber roller bottle.
3. Next, add in the patchouli, lavender, and ylang-ylang essential oils while focusing on your intentions.
4. Add the chamomile to fill any empty space.
5. Hold the bottle in your hands and envision energy wrapping around it. Charge it with your intentions. Say:

"With this oil, I blend and bless, well-being and feelings of gratefulness."

6. Wear it whenever you need to live in the moment and attract positivity

Ritual for Banishment of Internal Darkness

You will need:

- A clear glass bottle
- A small piece of clear quartz
- Enough spring water to fill the glass bottle
- A few drops of peppermint essential oil
- A few drops of lemon essential oil
- A few drops of sweet orange essential oil
- Strength card from an unused Tarot deck

Instructions:

1. Cast a sacred circle.
2. Fill the bottle with the spring water, add the drops of essential oils, and lastly add the clear quartz.

3. Cap the bottle.

4. Shake the bottle three times to mix and charge the elixir.

5. Place the bottle on the face-up Strength card and allow it to sit undisturbed for at least 10 minutes.

6. Open the bottle and remove the crystal.

7. Drink the elixir. As you drink, visualize the charged liquid entering your body and spreading from your stomach out; engulfing and transforming any and all pockets of darkness into radiant light.

8. Close the sacred circle.

Mental Wellness Spell

You will need:

- Soothing music (new age, classical, chants)
- A tumbled amethyst
- A tumbled rose quartz
- A blue candle with a candle holder
- Lavender Essential Oil

- Vanilla Essential Oil
- Sweet Orange Essential Oil

Instructions:

1. Center and ground your energy.
2. Begin to play your selected music.
3. Dress the blue candle with the essential oils.
4. Cast a sacred circle.
5. Light the dressed candle.
6. Sit in the center of the circle, holding one of the crystals in each hand. Close your eyes.
7. Breathe slowly and deeply. Inhale the scents from around you and allow them to calm and soothe your mind.
8. Rub the smooth crystals with your fingers.
9. Focus on your breathing. When your mind begins to wander, bring it back to focus with the word, "Peace."
10. When you begin to feel calm and your mind has quieted down, open your eyes, and snuff the candle.
11. Close the sacred circle.

Good luck Jar Spells

Spiritual Bath Spell for Good Luck

You will need:

- One white candle
- One sprig of Rue
- 3 leaves of Guinea hen weed
- One sprig of Rosemary

Why This Bath Works:

1. Rue is one of the most powerful herbs for spiritual healing because it has been used for a long time to protect people from psychic attacks, jealousy, curses, and more. Rue has been used this way for a long time. It is also very popular when cutting binds in love because Magic works that way. A rue bath makes you feel happy and rich.

2. Rosemary is a traditional kitchen witchcraft herb that can remove negative energies from food, water, the body and the home. It helps to start healing processes that deal with self-love, beauty, desire, and more.

3. Guinea Hen Weed grows in the Amazon rainforest and the Caribbean. It comes from Guinea Hen Weed. Shamans have used it for a long time to treat fevers anxiety and boost the immune system. This plant is made up of many antioxidants that fight infections and help with pain, so it's unique.

Road Opener Wiccan Candle Ritual

You will need:

- One white candle
- Bowl of water (regular drinking water)
- One incense stick
- One crystal or gemstone (pick one according to the day)

Instructions:

1. Make sure your items are on the altar in the correct order before you do this. They'll all face one of the four ways: Water facing West, Air facing East, Earth facing north and Fire facing South.

2. A candle should be lit to make the incense smell. The Air element has come into your ritual.

3. You want to rub your hands together for a few seconds until you feel warm energy. Then, visualize a ball of energy and hold your crystal. You are invoking the Earth element.

4. Light the candle so that you can call on the Fire element to come to you.

5. Gentle dip your finger in the water to feel like you're with the Water element. Water is like a mirror that can show you a different world. This transforming energy will remove all of the blocks.

6. Chant the following prayer to open the road: A prayer chant to open the road

7. An empty road comes to mind. As you see yourself moving forward, take a few minutes to think about where you want to go.

8. Take care of the candle at all times. If you have to leave the room, you can put out the candle and keep it going when you get back.

9. Toss the rest away once the candle has burned out and say "thank you." You should keep the crystal close to you to see it better. To use this spell's power, rub your hands together and hold it in your hands again.

'Bad Luck, Go Away!' Candle Spell to Remove a Curse

You will need:

- Salt
- One green candle
- Cinnamon powder

Instructions:

1. You can put the green candle on your shrine.
2. Spread some salt around it to make a circle that protects it. Say: good-luck-spell-incantation
3. The green candle is lit. Think about all the bad luck you've had. Say: go-away-bad-luck
4. Imagine that all the problems in your life are gone.
5. As soon as it has cooled down for 5 minutes, sprinkle the cinnamon powder over the salt.
6. It helps to think of that extra good luck as a bright light that comes to you as you picture all the good things you want to

happen in your life. Negative thoughts and memories should be erased and replaced with images of new chances.

7. Burn it all the way through.

Good Luck & Prosperity Cinnamon Spell

You will need:

- Cinnamon incense
- Wooden incense holder

Instructions:

1. Place the cinnamon incense stick on the wooden incense holder and light it. This will help you to smell better.
2. As many times as you want, say the following chant:
3. It's good luck. Prosperity Chant is a spell.
4. Take a deep breath and let the smoke from the cinnamon fill your home as you think about how it will clean and protect you from bad luck.

Magic Sun Sigil

You will need:

- Piece of paper
- One yellow candle
- Pen or pencil
- One incense stick or essential oil (such as Lemon, Lavender, Jasmine, Rosemary, Cinnamon, Peppermint).
- Your study books or course material

Instructions:

1. Make sure the incense is lit and take three deep breaths before you do anything else. Relax and have a good attitude. To ground yourself, you can make a circle or just sit still for a short time.

2. Take the piece of paper and draw a picture of the sun. In any way you want, or keep it simple: It doesn't have to be very big to work. You need to put the sun sigil on something to pass a test.

3. Light the yellow candle and say the spell: Using Spell to help me pass my test

4. See yourself, or the Sun's spiritual power, coming to help you. Giving you the strength, focus, and memory you need to do well on the test. Imagining the sun giving off its light will help you clear your mind so you can pass the exam.

5. People can meditate for a few minutes or pray to a solar deity when they have some time on their hands.

6. Put out the candle when you're ready. You can blow it out. Keep the drawing with you. In the test, it will be your lucky amulet.

Charge & Activate Talismans or Amulets

You will need:

- One small bowl of salt
- One white candle
- One glass of water (or your chalice)
- One incense stick (pick any aroma that speaks to you)

Instructions:

1. There is a candle and some incense that needs to be lit,
2. Stand facing North with the amulet in your hands.

3. Hold it over the salt and say the chant:

4. Amulet of blessing

5. Turn to the East and, while holding the amulet over the smoke from the incense, say: Consecrate an amulet.

6. When you turn to the South, hold the amulet over the flame of a candle, be careful not to burn it.

7. Finally, turn to the West, and hold your amulet over the water in the glass. Consecration of a water amulet:

8. As you hold the amulet aloft, say Amulet blessing. Out loud, say what your amulet is for.

9. Do not take off your amulet for the next five days.

Good Luck Spell Chant: Janus' New Beginnings

You will need:

- An old key
- One green candle
- Piece of paper
- One black candle

- Pen or pencil

Instructions:

1. Light the black candle and let it take in any negative thoughts you have about starting this new cycle, and then let them go away.

2. The green candle is lit. Take a deep breath and think about your goal for the ritual.

3. Use the pen to write down your goal on the paper. Do not be afraid to be as detailed as you need to be. You can write one word or a whole page of your thoughts.

4. Use your pen or pencil to outline the key on the paper. If you don't have a key, you can copy this one from Roman history. The key is a symbol of unlocking the doors of change. The Janus Key

5. Say this chant:

6. It's good luck. Spell out the words for Chant.

7. Some green candle wax should be poured on the picture of the key.

8. Meditate. Ensure the candle doesn't get too hot during the next few days. Make sure to keep the page in your book of

mirrors. Check back with it in about three months to see if you've achieved your goal.

Attract More Good Luck in the New Moon

You will need:

- Dish
- Coarse salt
- One white candle
- 7 red rose petals (dried or fresh)

Instructions:

1. The dish should be on your altar, so put it there. Use a handful of salt to make a circle around the dish to protect it.
2. Place seven petals of a red rose on top of the salt circle.
3. Light a white candle in the middle of the dish.
4. Sit down, breathe slowly, and let go. All the paths in your life should become clear, and all the doors should open for you.
5. This chant is for when you're ready: People who are grateful for the help the moon can cast spells.

6. Do the same thing with the same ingredients and candle for seven days. On the last day, let it go.

Protection Jar Spells

Protecting Home and Heart

This spell is ideal for when you first move into a new living space: you can ensure that any negative energy put out by previous occupants is dispelled, and reassure your own sense of safety. To fortify, recast the spell each year on the anniversary of your initial move-in.

When to Perform:

When needed

How long it takes:

Two days

You will need:

- 1 black taper candle
- 1 white taper candle
- Lemon and rose essential oils
- 4 small glass jars
- Dried lavender, basil, salt and rice

Instructions:

1. The day before you intend to cast the spell, thoroughly smudge your entire house. Get up at sunrise (an auspicious time) and tidy everything before doing a sage smudging.

2. Fill each of your jars with lavender, basil, salt, and rice, respectively, and place them in the four cardinal directions in your home—on a windowsill, if possible—or out in the garden, if you have one. The lavender brings peacefulness to the household, while the basil offers protection; the salt wards-off negative energies, while the rice is thought to bring good fortune. Let the moonlight charge these containers overnight.

3. The next day, preferably at sunrise, arrange your jars in the four cardinal directions on your altar with the candles in between. Light your black candle to banish evil, your white candle to purify. Anoint the black candle with lemon essential oil for protection, your white candle with rose oil for blessings.

4. Cast your spell with clear intentions: *"Bless this house, with peace and love. Cleanse all that should be rid of. Protect all those dwelling here, to keep us close, safe, and dear."*

5. Let the candles burn down entirely, and bury the wax remnants near your foundation. You can keep the jars on your window sills for a few weeks, if you like, and/or you can use the contents to conjure up some magically enhanced potions and meals. Some practitioners don't use the herbs or

other edible ingredients that have been a part of their spells, but I find it perfectly acceptable, not only because it infuses some magic into what I eat, but also because it keeps with the spirit of economy and recycling that is a part of any good spellcaster's philosophy.

Safe Voyages: a Protection Spell for Travel

This is a quick and easy spell that you can perform whenever you're going on a trip.

When to perform:

When needed: best on Wednesday before you embark on your journey

How long it takes:

As long as it takes the candle to burn down

You will need:

- 1 white taper candle
- Rosemary essential oil
- Rose quartz crystal

Instructions:

1. Consider smudging your entire house, rather than just your altar for this spell. This will also banish negative energies in your home, keeping everything positive for your return.

2. Anoint your candle and the crystal with the protective rosemary oil, light the candle, and cast your spell: "*I call upon the spirit of the moon, to help me reach my destination soon. I want my trip happy and safe to be, for all involved, including me.*" Pass the crystal through the flame three times while you repeat your incantation.

3. Carry the crystal with you on your journey. Store the remnants of the candle somewhere safe until you return, then bury them close to your home.

Avoiding Accidents: a Prevention Spell

Essentially, this spell teaches you how to make a talisman that you can carry with you for general safety. I keep this pouch of ingredients in my car and thus far it's worked like a literal charm!

When to perform:

During a full moon

How long it takes:

As long as it takes for the candle to burn

You will need:

- 1 black taper candle
- Small pouch
- Dried sage, rosemary, and salt
- Amethyst crystal
- Personal item (see steps below)

Instructions:

1. Cleanse your altar before you begin, and if you have the time, charge the crystal in the moonlight before you cast your spell.

2. Place your candle in the center of your space, and light it while reciting your incantation: *"Here I ask that safe I'll be, no matter how wild and free. Use these things to protect me from harm, infuse them with power to work like a charm."*

3. As you let your candle burn, fill the pouch with your ingredients: a teaspoon or two of each of your protection herbs, along with the salt; add the amethyst crystal for soothing fear; put in a personal item that you feel has magical properties to you. For example, I use whiskers from my cats (not pulled out, of course. I collect them as they are shed). But you can use anything you feel is a personal good luck charm.

4. Keep the talismanic pouch in your car or in your purse or briefcase so that it watches over you at all times.

Legal Relief: a Spell to Win a Court Case

As anyone knows who has ever faced any kind of legal snafu, this can take a toll on your peace of mind (not to mention your time and energy). This spell can help you "sweeten the deal," as it were, and bring positive results to any kind of court case you find yourself negotiating.

When to perform:

Seven days before the court date

How long it takes:

As long as it takes for the candle to burn

You will need:

- 1 brown tea candle
- Small jar
- Honey
- Black mustard seeds, cayenne pepper, and galangal root
- Pen and paper (optional)

Instructions:

1. Cleanse your space before you begin. You can put this together in your kitchen, if you like, after a good sage smudging.

2. Pour the honey into the jar, and add a tablespoon of black mustard seeds to confuse your opponents, a couple of pinches of cayenne pepper to ward off negative energy, and three slices of fresh galangal root (or a couple of teaspoons powdered) for good luck and protection.

3. Light your brown tea candle and recite your incantation: *"Keep me grounded and help me win, vanquish my enemies and save my skin!"* Let the candle burn all the way down, then place the remnants in your spell jar and keep it in an auspicious place until the results are in.

Conjuring Peace: a Spell for a Happy Household

This spell attracts the positive energies needed to keep everyone in your home getting along with one another. The spell jar is intended to sit at a central place in your home, where it will draw on all the fundamental elements to keep the positive energy flowing.

When to perform:

Any time during a waxing moon, though a Friday is thought to be best

How long it takes:

As long as it takes for the candles to burn

You will need:

- 2 blue tea candles
- 2 yellow tea candles
- Vanilla essential oil
- Small glass jar
- Dried basil, lavender, thyme, catnip, and lemon peel
- Lapis lazuli stone
- Rose quartz stone
- A couple of drops of sun-charged water

Instructions:

1. Cleanse your altar space, as per usual, and prepare your spell jar. Add a tablespoon each of basil for protection and luck, lavender for peace, thyme for joy, catnip for attraction, and lemon peel for happiness.

2. Anoint the stones with a couple of drops of sun-charged water (water that has been exposed to full sunlight for three hours), then place them in the jar: the lapis lazuli soothes

and invites intuition, while the rose quartz promotes friendship and romantic love.

3. Place your candles in the four cardinal directions—the blue at north/earth and west/water, the yellow at south/fire and east/air—and anoint them with soothing vanilla essential oil.

4. As you light the candles, cast your spell: *"Here I ask for this home to have peace, for all negative energy and strife to cease. I invite much happiness and joy to all who dwell here, girl and boy."*

5. Let the candles burn down, and bury their remains at the foundation of your home.

Vanquishing Visitors: a Spell to Get Rid of Unwanted Guests

We all know what it's like to have the obtuse guest who doesn't realize it's time to leave, whether that be an annoying uncle at the holidays or an old friend who's crashing on your couch. Here's a simple, but gentle, banishment spell to restore your privacy.

When to perform:

When needed

How long it takes:

As long as it takes for the candle to burn

You will need:

- 1 black taper candle
- Lemon or mint essential oil
- Black pepper, cayenne, and cinnamon

Instructions:

1. Cleanse your altar or space. You might consider smudging the area in which the unwanted guest has been sleeping (if you can do so while they aren't around).

2. Anoint your black banishment candle with lemon or mint oil; both provide purification and protection for your space. Mix together your spices, about a tablespoon of each, and roll your candle in them: black pepper provides stamina and courage; cayenne sends away negative energy; cinnamon brings protection.

3. Light your candle and recite your incantation: *"Hear me now as I ask my guest to go, give me peace and end this woe."* Repeat this seven times as you watch the candle burn.

4. Be sure to get rid of the remnants as soon as possible: this might be an occasion for a handy toilet flush!

Under Your Thumb No More: a Spell to Free Yourself from Influence

If you've ever been involved in an unhealthy relationship, whether a romantic relationship or friendship went sour or even a domineering family member, this spell can help you free yourself from that negative influence. You might also try casting a decision-making spell, as well, or a confidence spell to get you back to your own clarity of thinking.

When to perform:

Any time during a waning moon

How long it takes:

As long as it takes to burn and scatter ashes

You will need:

- 2 white taper candles
- 1 red or purple taper candle
- Pen and paper
- Flameproof bowl or dish

Instructions:

1. Cleanse your altar space, as per usual, and line up your candles with the red or purple candle in between your white candles. Choose red if the person of influence has controlled

you with passion or anger; choose purple if that influence has been more psychological or spiritual. The white candles will pull that energy from the central candle, purifying your intentions.

2. Write the person's name on the piece of paper and set it alight while you cast your spell: *"I ask that you step away from my life, freeing me from this constant strife. I reclaim my mind and soul, rejecting your influence and becoming whole."*

3. When your candles and paper have burned, scatter the ashes to the winds, bury the remnants of the white candles somewhere that brings you joy, and send the red or purple candle away in the water.

Karmic Returns: a Spell to Reverse Evil Sent to You

One of the most fundamental tenets of working magic is that you never wish harm to others. If you do, that karmic energy will return to you threefold. If you suspect someone has been engaging in this kind of magic against you, then you can return it to them—and let them rue the day they expelled that negative nonsense!

When to perform:

Start or end at the full moon

How long it takes:

About 10 minutes a day for nine days

You will need:

- 1 black pillar candle
- 1 white pillar candle
- 1 red pillar candle
- Cinnamon essential oil
- Penknife

Instructions:

1. Cleanse your space well; this spell requires a lot of power behind it.

2. Prepare your candles: pick out some runes to carve into each candle. A pentacle is a banishing rune, which can work, or the Algiz for protection in general (when rendered upside down, this rune also constitutes a warning), or the Eihwaz for defense. Depictions of all of these can be found online. Alternately, you can carve your own symbology onto the candles, according to what works best for you. This can be as simple as carving your name into the white candle, your opponent's name into the black candle, and the offending deed into the red candle.

3. Arrange your candles in a triangle, with the white candle at the apex and anoint with cinnamon oil, which brings both energy and protection to your spell.

4. Cast your spell: *"I send back evil your way, three times three. Your bad intentions won't stay with me, as I return them to you, three times three."* Recite the incantation three times, then snuff the candles.

5. Repeat the spell each day (ideally at the same time) for nine days.

Love Jar Spells

Gimme Love Spell Jar

You will need:

- Pink food coloring for romance
- Dried or fresh lavender for love and protection
- Orange food coloring for attraction
- Dried or fresh red or pink roses for love
- Cinnamon for protection
- Paper
- One pen/marker with orange ink
- White sugar for sweetness
- One pink candle

Instructions:

1. Fill two bowls with half-white sugar. Add one drop of pink food coloring to one and one drop of orange food coloring to the other one. The sugar in each bowl should be the same color.

2. With a pen and paper, write down the things you want in the person you want to meet. Then put the paper in the bottom of your jar.

3. With a mortar and pestle, mix together the roses and lavender while you think about how you want to find love.

4. Stack pink sugar, herb mix, and orange sugar until the jar is full.

5. Sprinkle a little cinnamon on top to make it look like love and happiness are on top.

6. A pink candle can be used to burn over the top of the jar.

New Year, New Me Clarity Jar

You will need:

- Airtight jar
- Whole cloves for clarity
- Sea salt (big grain) for protection and cleansing
- Mint leaves for communication
- Ground coffee to dispel negative thoughts
- Whole rosemary sprigs for mental clarity

- Cinnamon sticks for protection and mental focus
- One orange candle for stimulating your mental energy

Instructions:

1. In your jar, put each ingredient on top of the other, and think about how you will use it.
2. Seal the jar and light an orange candle on top.

Spell to Open Roads to Love

You will need:

- Paper and pencil
- One pink candle
- Candle holder or dish
- 3 dried white flowers (e.g., daisies, carnations, lilies, tulips, daffodils, or others)
- Incense (e.g., cinnamon, jasmine, roses or ylang-ylang)
- Your cauldron or any fireproof container

- Essential oil (e.g., cinnamon, clove, jasmine, linden flower, myrtle, orange, palmarosa, rose, vanilla or yarrow)

Instructions:

1. It's time to light the incense and let its scent fill the room.

2. It's time for you to dress up your candle with the essential oil so that you can open the door to the powerful love that changes everything. Do this and say: Putting love spells on the candle

3. Make sure the candle is lit and put it on the candle stand or a dish.

4. Take one of the white flowers and gently peel off each petal one by one, making sure not to damage them. During this, breathe slowly and say the following: Fire-Flower-Spell

5. Use all three flowers, and put the petals in a pot. Do not worry or think about anything during this time.

6. On the paper, write your full name.

7. It is safe to light the piece of paper with the candle flame and put it in the cauldron.

8. It's OK to let the candle burn and put its ashes in the flowerpot as you say. Thanks.

9. Take the ashes and the last petals from the cauldron and bury them in the ground (in a garden or flower pot).

Self-Love & Spiritual Acceptance

You will need:

- 8 rose petals (fresh or dried)
- One white candle
- 2 tablespoons of Cinnamon powder

Instructions:

1. In a pot, put 4 cups of water. Then, put the pot on a stove over high heat.
2. Add the rose petals and cinnamon to the dough and mix it well.
3. Turn off the heat when it starts to boil. Let it sit for about 15 minutes before you start to eat it
4. Meanwhile, take a quick shower to clean your body. Then, fill the tub with warm water and get in there.
5. It's time to light a white candle. Add the rose petals, cinnamon, and water to the water.

6. As you pour the water on your body and face, think about why your heart is hurting. You should not only think about what other people have done to you. You should also think about how you have treated your own body.

7. Thank yourself and ask that all bad thoughts go away. Take note of the things that your emotions are trying to say. Your fears will help you figure out what to do, Self-Love-Spell-Bath

8. Get out of the tub when you're ready and do what makes you happy.

Self-Love Bath

Bath magic is ideal for cleansing away old energy and for allowing new, nurturing energy to take root. This spell is perfect for generating more self-love for your physical, mental, emotional, psychological, and spiritual self.

When to perform this spell:

On a Monday, Friday, or during a full moon

Time to allot for the spell:

30 minutes

Where to perform the spell:

Bathroom

You will need:

- 1 cup Epsom salt
- 3 drops jasmine essential oil
- 3 drops rose essential oil
- Lighter or matches
- Pink pillar candle
- Rose quartz crystal

Instructions:

1. Cleanse your bathroom.
2. Fill your bathtub with warm or hot water.
3. Add the Epsom salt and jasmine and rose essential oils.
4. As the tub fills, light the candle and set it in a safe location nearby.
5. Hold the rose quartz in your dominant hand and soak in the bath for 20 minutes. Focus on the things you love about yourself. Feel the bathwater infuse your body and the rose quartz with love and healing energies.

6. After 20 minutes, drain the bath and blow out the candle.

7. Whenever you need a boost of self-love, light the candle and hold the rose quartz.

Getting Over Love Spell

This spell will help you move on from past love. The ideal time to cast this spell is after a full moon, once the moon begins to wane back into the darkness of the new moon.

When to perform this spell:

During a waning moon

Time to allot for the spell:

15 minutes

Where to perform the spell:

Altar

You will need:

- 3 drops clove essential oil
- 1 tablespoon olive oil
- Small dish

- Black pillar candle

- Lighter or matches

- Pen and paper

- Large bowl

- Small bowl

- About ½ cup water

Instructions:

1. Cleanse your altar.

2. Mix the clove essential oil and olive oil in a small dish. Using your fingers, anoint your black candle. Be careful not to get oil on the wick.

3. Light the candle and focus on your intentions to cut ties with your ex-lover.

4. Write a goodbye message to the feelings that no longer serve you. Put the message in a large bowl.

5. Fill a small bowl with water and place your hands into it, cleansing away pain, anger, and resentment.

6. Lift some water out of the bowl with your hands and throw it on the paper, enforcing your goodbye.

7. Squeeze the paper and discard it, removing it from your life.

8. Whenever you feel old feelings returning, light your anointed candle.

Custom Love Sigil

Creating a custom love sigil is fun and creative! This sigil is perfect for drawing more attention to you from your love interest. It's also the perfect way to illuminate your true feelings.

When to perform this spell:

On a Friday or during a new moon

Time to allot for the spell:

10 minutes

Where to perform the spell:

Altar

You will need:

- 2 sheets of paper
- Pen with red ink

Instructions:

1. Cleanse your altar.

2. Write your name and your love interest's name on one of the sheets of paper with a red pen.

3. Deconstruct the letters of the names into their basic strokes, like curves, dots, dashes, and lines. Draw these strokes below the names on the same paper.

4. Still, on the same sheet of paper, combine the strokes to form the outline of a shape. This could be a square, a heart, a cross, or a triangle. Place any remaining circles, arcs, and dashes along the lines or around the shape. This shape is your love sigil.

5. Redraw your love sigil, now coded with your intentions, on the second sheet of paper. Carry it with you.

Restore Love Knot Spell

Did you have an argument with your loved one that you regret? Do you want to bring your romance back to the beginning? This spell is perfect for returning the energy of your relationship back to how it was when the love was pure and new.

When to perform this spell:

On a Monday or during a new moon

Time to allot for the spell:

45 to 60 minutes

Where to perform the spell:

Altar

You will need:

- Desire Incense or Positivity Incense
- Charcoal disc and heat-proof dish (optional)
- 3 red tea light candles
- Lighter or matches
- 2 (12-inch) pieces of string in different colors

Instructions:

1. Cleanse your altar.
2. Burn your Desire or Positivity Incense. If your incense is loose, burn it on a charcoal disc on a heat-proof dish. Set up the candles in a triangular configuration.
3. Light the candles and focus on your intention of restoring love.

4. Hold the two strings together and tie a simple overhand knot at one end. As you do this, say, "Knot of love, revive what has vanished."

5. Tie another knot and say, "Knot of passion, bring back the delight."

6. Tie a third knot and say, "Knot of adoration, renew what was damaged."

7. Tie a fourth and final knot and say, "Knot of desire, mend and rewrite."

8. Allow the candles to burn while you meditate, visualizing the love you want to be restored. Continue until 45 to 60 minutes have passed.

Burning Heartbreak Spell

Burn away heartbreak using the element of fire. This spell uses photographs and lemon balm, which is known for its healing properties. It will help you recover from the emotional pain of a broken relationship.

When to perform this spell:

On a Monday or during a dark moon

Time to allot for the spell:

30 to 45 minutes

Where to perform the spell:

Altar or outdoor firepit

You will need:

- Outdoor firepit, if outside
- Fire-safe bowl, if indoors at your altar
- Lighter or matches
- 2 photographs, one of you and another of the person who broke your heart
- A small handful dried lemon balm
- Sea salt (optional)

Instructions:

1. Cleanse your altar or outdoor firepit area.
2. If performing the spell indoors, use a lighter to ignite the edge of each photo before placing it inside your fire-safe bowl. If spellcasting outside, you may toss each photo one at a time into the fire. As the photographs burn, say: "With this photo, I ease my sorrow; with this fire, I burn away this grief; with these ashes, I take away this pain."

3. When you have burned both of your photos, toss the lemon balm into the fire or into the bowl.

4. Optional: Collect some of the ash from the fire and mix it with sea salt to create a powerful nonedible black salt that can be sprinkled or thrown around you to banish negative emotions in the future.

Mending Heartbreak Talisman

This spell will teach you how to create a talisman that will assist your heart's healing. Your talisman must be worn at all times. This recipe uses cayenne pepper, which provides support during separations and emotional heartache.

When to perform this spell:

On a Monday or during a dark moon

Time to allot for the spell:

15 minutes

Where to perform the spell:

Altar

You will need:

- Pinch of cayenne pepper

- Black or white votive or pillar candle
- Lighter or matches
- Necklace

Instructions:

1. Cleanse your altar.
2. Sprinkle the cayenne pepper on the top of the candle to anoint it.
3. Light the candle and visualize its mending properties.
4. Move your necklace through the candle's smoke as you say: "Necklace of healing, fill the void of my broken heart as I imbue you with energy and feeling; support me in creating my restart."
5. Allow your power to infuse the necklace, charging it for use.
6. Repeat the spell every few months to recharge the talisman. You may use the same candle.

Charm for Attracting Quality Relationships

This spell draws on both the attracting and protective qualities of coriander for a balanced approach to attracting new potential partners into your life.

This is particularly good for those who seem to have no trouble attracting admirers, but plenty of trouble in the relationships that develop. With the energy of coriander, people who are ultimately no good for you will not make it into your sphere of awareness, while people who present a positive, healthy, compatible match will have a clear path to you.

Adding rose quartz to the mix enhances the positive vibration of the spell. Be sure to get whole seeds rather than coriander powder, since you'll be carrying the herb with you.

You will need:

- 13 whole coriander seeds
- 1 small rose quartz
- 1 small drawstring bag or piece of cloth
- 1 red or pink ribbon
- 1 work candle (for atmosphere—optional)

Instructions:

1. Light the candle, if using.

2. Arrange the coriander seeds in a circle around the rose quartz.

3. Close your eyes and visualize the feeling of being completely at peace with a partner who loves you for exactly who you are.

4. When you have a lock on this feeling, open your eyes, focus on the rose quartz, and say the following (or similar) words: "I draw to me nothing less than healthy, balanced love."

5. Now collect the coriander seeds, placing them one at a time into the drawstring bag or cloth. (It's best to start with the seed at the southern-most part of the circle and move clockwise.)

6. Add the rose quartz, close the bag or cloth, and secure with the ribbon.

7. Bring the charm with you whenever you're feeling like taking a chance on love—especially when you go out in public.

Romance Attraction Smudge

This is a fun, simple ritual for enhancing the atmosphere in your home or any space where you'd like to encourage romance!

You will need:

- 1 red candle
- Sprig of dried lavender or lavender-only smudge stick
- Rose essential oil (optional)
- 1 feather (optional)

Instructions:

1. Anoint the candle with a drop or two of the rose oil, if using. Wipe away any excess oil from your fingers, and then light the candle.

2. Ignite the lavender sprig or smudge stick from the candle flame as you say the following (or similar) words: "Loving lavender, creative fire, charge this space with love's desire."

3. Starting at a point in the northern part of the room, move in a clockwise circle, fanning the lavender smoke with the feather (if using) or your hand, so that it spreads throughout the room as much as possible. If you like, you can repeat the words of power above as a chant as you go.

4. Leave the lavender to burn out on its own in a fire-proof dish, if possible—otherwise, you can extinguish it gently in a potted plant or bowl of sand.

Stellar First Date Confidence Charm

If you're the type who gets nervous before meeting a potential love interest for the first time, this spell is for you.

Simply carry the charm with you in your pocket or purse—you may want to enclose it in a drawstring bag or cloth if you're carrying it with other items to keep it intact.

Keep in mind that the focus here is on your own confidence and sense of self-love no matter what the *other person is like.* If you have a good time, no matter what the outcome, then the spell has been a success.

You will need:

- One pink or white ribbon, about seven inches
- One little piece of carnelian or tiger's eye
- Sea salt
- One work candle (optional)
- One little drawstring bag or piece of cloth (optional)

Instructions:

1. Light the candle, if using.

2. Lay out the ribbon on your altar or workspace.

3. Create a circle of sea salt around the ribbon—this will concentrate the energy of the spell around the charm.

4. Place the stone on the ribbon, and say the following (or similar) words:

   "My confidence radiates from within
   I am comfortable in my own skin
   This meeting of souls will be a pleasure
   I charm this stone for extra measure."

5. Tie the ribbon gently around the stone and secure it with a knot.

6. Now go out and have fun meeting someone new!

Ritual Bath for a Blind Date

Whether you're on a blind date set up by a friend, or taking the plunge into the world of online dating, it can be nerve-wracking to meet someone new.

This spell makes it nearly impossible not to have a good time, by sublimating nervousness and promoting self-confidence, which will improve the energy of the encounter no matter what the outcome. Indeed, you will enjoy yourself even if it's clear by the end that there won't be a second date!

You will need:

- One tsp. to one tbsp. hibiscus
- One tsp. to one tbsp. chamomile
- One tsp. to one. tbsp. coltsfoot or red clover
- Two to three tbsp. Himalayan salt or sea salt
- Five drops of lavender essential oil
- One citrine, aventurine, or tiger's eye
- Candle(s) for atmosphere

Instructions:

1. Run the bath until the tub is a quarter of the way full, and add the salt.
2. When the tub is halfway full, place the crystal of your choice in the water, and add the oil.
3. When the bath is almost full, add the herbs.

4. Light the candle(s), turn off any artificial lighting in the bathroom, and climb in.

5. Relax and consciously release any anxiety you may be feeling about meeting this new person. Also, release any attachments you may be feeling to the desired outcome.

6. Stay in the bath for at least 20 minutes. If you can, remain in the tub while draining the water, as the energy of the herbs and crystal tends to have a stronger effect that way.

7. Bring the crystal with you on the date, and have a good time!

Rose Attraction Potion

This potion is ideal for attracting potential new suitors or admirers into your life. It involves easy-to-find herbs and tools that you likely already have in your home. A rose is the best flower to use in this recipe due to its association with love.

When to perform this spell:

On a Friday or during a waxing moon

Time to allot for the spell:

15 minutes

Where to perform the spell:

Kitchen

You will need:

- Small pot
- 1 cup water
- 1 teaspoon dried rose petals
- 1 teaspoon dried hibiscus flowers
- 1 teaspoon dried lavender flowers
- Pinch of cinnamon
- Muslin cloth or strainer
- Cup for drinking

Instructions:

1. Cleanse your kitchen.
2. In a small pot, boil the water as you set your intentions.
3. Remove the pot from the heat. Place the rose petals, hibiscus, lavender, and cinnamon one at a time into the pot. As you do this, repeat the words "Infuse, imbue, impart, immerse" four times.

4. Slowly stir the mixture as you visualize the energy of attraction wrapping around the herbs in the pot. Allow the potion to steep for 10 minutes.

5. Strain the potion into a cup and drink.

Valentine's Day Jar Spell

You will need:

- Love oil
- Salt
- One jar with a lid
- Honey
- One candle (pink, red or white)
- Flower petals (optional)

Instructions:

1. Dress the candle with love oil. As you do this, think about bringing love to you as you put the oil on the candle and point it at yourself.

2. To put the candle on your altar, you should put it in a candle holder.

3. In the jar, put 5 drops of the oil in, and add 1 tablespoon of honey. To make the jar look pretty, you can put flower petals, such as roses, inside of it.

4. Make sure the lid is on the jar and put it on your altar next to the candle.

5. Sprinkle a little salt on your shrine. You can put salt around the candle and the jar to keep them safe. Any kind of salt you have in your kitchen will work. You can use it.

6. As you light the candle, think about what you want to bring in. Think about the things that make this person unique (with or without thinking of any specific person). This is Valentine's Day Love Spell Chant.

7. Chant the chant over and over again like a mantra and then go into meditation; look down to find a love-themed meditative song to listen to while you clean your body in the bath.

8. Burn it all the way through. If you need to leave the room, put it out and then start it again when you get back. Finish the candle next week.

Sugar Jar Love Spell

You will need:

- Jar
- Sugar
- Hibiscus, Rose, Lavender, Chamomile, Jasmine, Cinnamon, Orange, Lemon, Basil, Rosemary, Vanilla, and Oregano are some herbs and essential oils that you can use. You can choose any combination of them.
- Small piece of paper
- Red ink pen
- Rose quartz
- Pink or Red candle

Instructions:

1. Light a candle.
2. What you write on your paper will depend on what you want:
3. If you want to keep your relationship strong or attract a specific person, write your partner's name and birth date on paper. Draw a circle around it.

4. In the search for love, write down a few things you want your future partner to have.

5. In the present tense, write your name and what you need to be proud of, or what you want for yourself.

6. Using a few drops of wax from your candle, seal your paper into a scroll. You could also wrap the scroll with red or pink ribbon or thread if you'd rather. Add the scroll to the glass jar.

7. Add your ingredients and the rose quartz to fill the jar and cover the scroll.

8. Take a small amount of the sugar mix and sprinkle it around your candle.

9. Seal your jar and hold it up to the flame while you say:

"Fire that flickers and burns bright.

Sweet dreams: I'll send you some tonight.

People are starting to fall in love with each other under this moon, which shines and glows. A heart is getting sweeter, and things are going to change soon.

Earth, Wind, Fire and Sea: "This Is My Will, and So It Is!"

6. It's best to let the candle go out on its own (or extinguish it if planning to re-use it). Keep the jar next to your bed while you sleep.

7. Light a candle and repeat the spell once a week with a small pinch of your sugar mixture. Do this every week.

Lovers' Bind Rune

Preserve or attract a loving relationship with the help of this bind rune. Bind runes are made by combining two or more runes into a single shape. To perform this spell, find a flat stone that calls to you. You'll use this stone to house your bind rune.

When to perform this spell:

On a Friday or during a new moon

Time to allot for the spell:

15 minutes

Where to perform the spell:

Altar

You will need:

Sleep Jar Spells

Divining Dreams: a Spell for Good Sleep

This spell should help you get a solid night's sleep. If you want to invite dreams, then add a stick of frankincense or lavender incense to burn during the spell.

When to Perform:

Anytime you need deep sleep

How long it takes:

As long as it takes the candle to burn down

You will need:

- 1 blue tea candle
- Amethyst or smoke quartz crystal

Instructions:

1. Perform this spell directly in your bedroom, and prepare yourself and the room for good sleep. Obviously, you want to cleanse the space thoroughly, as usual, but you also want to invest in some more practical aids for good sleep. Put fresh, clean sheets on your bed, have a comfy blanket and your

favorite pillow handy, turn off screens and keep the lighting dim, and consider playing some sleep-inducing music.

2. When you are ready for bed, light your candle first and recite your incantation, with your crystal in your hand. The crystal is representative of the moon itself, inviting nighttime serenity. State your intentions clearly: *"Here in my hand, I hold the moon, so its calming light will soothe me soon."*

3. Let your tea candle burn down safely, as you tuck the crystal under your pillow and yourself into bed.

Negating Nightmares: Another Spell for Good Sleep

This spell can also be aided with herbal potions that help you sleep soundly (or just some unfussy chamomile tea), as nightmares are often caused by an agitated mind. If your nightmares come from a psychic interference or some deep well of anxiety or trauma, you may need to perform this spell fairly regularly for it to produce results. Casting it in conjunction with anxiety spells or other banishing spells can also increase its efficacy.

When to Perform:

When necessary for peaceful sleep

How long it takes:

About 10-15 minutes before bedtime

You will need:

- 1 black taper candle
- 1 silver ribbon
- 1 silver coin

Instructions:

1. As with the previous spell, prepare your bedroom not only with cleansing or smudging but also with practical considerations (clean sheets, comfy blanket and pillow, soothing music, and so on).

2. Tie your silver ribbon around your black candle: the silver symbolizes spiritual awakening and higher thinking, as it binds the banishing candle.

3. Hold your coin in your left hand as you light your candle and cast your spell: *"These dreams that come before the dawn, make not me a frightened pawn. I ask the moon, so calm and sure to bring me peace just like a cure."*

4. Let the candle burn for a few minutes, as you visualize a peaceful scene or a previous happy dream. Put the coin on your windowsill, snuff the black candle, and tie the ribbon around your wrist before bed. You can reuse these magical tools for three nights in a row, if necessary.

Conclusion

Bottle spells are a time-honored tradition in witchcraft and folk magic and are a versatile and powerful form of spell work. If mastered, they can help you to achieve success with real-world results, such as getting rid of unwanted situations, attaining love, or getting a pay raise at your work.

Do not get discouraged if your spells do not work at first; every witch has to fail in order to learn and develop her powers and magic skills. Just keep trying and adjusting. Have faith; with time, you will feel more powerful in your practice, further your spirituality, and be able to craft your destiny.

I really hope you have enjoyed this collection. White magic is a fascinating subject, and, of course, there is still so much you can learn about it.

If you want your spells and rituals to be effective, never forget to practice with an open mind, with great respect, and, above all, for the right reason.

Printed in Great Britain
by Amazon